The Safeguarding Jigsaw

Your place in the child protection process

KATE YOUNG

Copyright © 2016 Katherine T. Young

All rights reserved.

No part of this document may be reproduced or transmitted in any form whatsoever without the express written permission of the author.

The information presented herein presents the view of the author at the date of publication. The author reserves the right to alter and update her opinion based on new conditions as they arise. This publication is for informational purposes only. If advice concerning legal, health or related matters is needed, the services of a fully qualified professional should be sought.

ISBN:1540355934
ISBN-13:9781540355935

DEDICATION

This book is dedicated to the man who, through a conversation he cannot remember, set me on the path to the world of child protection. Thank you Dad, for everything.

CONTENTS

	Acknowledgments	i
	Foreword	1
	Introduction	3
1	Sharing Information	4
2	Getting Over The Nerves	9
3	Where Are We Headed?	18
4	Disclosures And Referrals	23
5	Strategy Meetings	31
6	Initial Enquiries/Section 47 Enquiries	39
7	Child In Need Process	48
8	Child Protection Conferences	54
9	Public Law Outline Process	61
10	Care Proceedings	65
	Conclusion	74

ACKNOWLEDGMENTS

Thanks go to Kate Cobb, for her guidance and support. Thanks also to Sharon Gaskin and her tribe for keeping me on track. The wonderful Kirsty Lyons for her fabulous eye for detail, and the marvelous Steve Cooke for his wonders with the cover. For the encouragement and never ending support, my parents. Finally, for his never ending encouragements and patience, my husband, Alan.

FOREWORD

The importance of safeguarding children and vulnerable people cannot be overstated. I strongly believe that as a society and as humans, we have a moral and ethical duty of care for others. In the UK this is also enshrined in law.

However, it can sometimes be confusing for practitioners who don't work with safeguarding issues every day as to what is a legal duty or how we should act in certain circumstances. And this is why this book is such a valuable resource for practitioners working with children. Kate explains clearly the legislation involved but, more importantly, the role of practitioners within the system. Her advice is not just about knowing the legislation and bureaucracy, but is also focused on how you – as an individual – can prepare for a variety of circumstances.

Safeguarding guidelines are updated on a regular basis, so knowing you are up to date and that, crucially, you know the rationale behind your actions can make all the difference to the outcomes for that child and family. Kate's book will help you to navigate around the world of safeguarding and disclosures and be confident that you are doing the very best for the children in your care.

From the minute you start reading this book, there is a wealth of practical information, which you can clearly see is based on years of real-life experience. Obviously it is to be hoped that you will never have to be involved with a serious safeguarding case, but as children's advocates you should always be aware of the best course of action for the children in your care. Having this knowledge in advance means that if the worst should ever happen, you are fully prepared and able to swing into action immediately, without wasting precious time.

Safeguarding as a jigsaw is also a perfect analogy. Until all the pieces of the jigsaw are assembled, you cannot see the full picture, although you may be able to make professional judgements on the puzzle piece that you do have. The gathering together of the pieces of information and then interlocking them to make an unambiguous picture is the crux of good safeguarding procedure. This book explains how to do all this for you, with the added benefit of being practical as well.

Altogether this is an essential book for anyone working with children.

Kathy Brodie

INTRODUCTION

I decided to write this book after many years of working with professionals who are new to the world of child protection. Many were on the edges of this world, peering in through dark glasses. To the uninitiated, the world of child protection can seem cold, scary and intimidating.

Through my discussions, and training sessions, a picture emerged. Many professionals were unaware of the vital information they held within their heads or organisation.

They were unaware of how important these patterns of behaviour were or how crucial one child's reaction to a particular situation could be.

In essence, they were holding key pieces of a child's personal jigsaw, but did not know what it was or how to share it.

This book is your pocket guide to navigating every step. It will help you tackle each stage with confidence. You will see how you fit into the child protection process and how your piece of the jigsaw will be used through the child protection process.

1 SHARING INFORMATION

Sharing information is crucial in child protection. The only way anyone will ever get the full picture of a child's life is by information being shared. Everyone who knows the child will have a little (or big) piece of that child's life jigsaw. Every teacher, doctor, sports coach, gym teacher, health visitor, social worker, family support worker, parent, extended family member and friend; each person knows something about that child. No one person will hold the full picture. Instead, every person will hold a piece of the jigsaw.

Think of that jigsaw as the child's life.

There will be pieces around their home life. This will include their siblings, their parents and their extended family. It will include their relationships with those people, how many times a week they see them, and how they interact and respond to each other.

There will be pieces around their schooling and education. Big pieces will include their attendance, relationships with peers and teachers, how well they are doing, their progress, their self-care skills (depending on their age) etc. The smaller pieces may be their presentation, their punctuality, their engagement in classes. Teachers may also notice the smaller pieces of the jigsaw; for example, patterns of behaviour, marks to their body, comments made in a seemingly throw away fashion. These smaller pieces can often be the key indicators something is not right.

Health professionals will hold pieces, in respect of the number of appointments attended or missed. Or whether immunisations have been done or key appointments have been completed. They may notice that explanations for attendances at surgeries or hospitals are following a pattern, or that explanations given don't quite match up to the injuries or symptoms they are seeing. Each of these is a part of the child's jigsaw.

Out of school workers can also hold key information. A parent may blame an injury, mark or bruise on an activity. If you know it did not happen during your sessions then that is part of the jigsaw also. Sometimes children feel more comfortable sharing information with someone outside of their school or their family. You can be seen as a safe person to talk to, someone who won't tell parents or anyone else.

Each person in a child's life will hold something of that child's story. A teacher can't know what happened during an out of school activity unless they are told. Equally, a GP can't know what has happened at hospital unless it is recorded in the medical notes or information is passed on to them from another professional.

If these professionals who see the child on a regular basis can't see the full picture, then neither can the police or children's social care.

The police and children's social care do not act in isolation. They rely on information being shared.

Information can be shared in a variety of ways. The most common is through a referral. I'll share more on that in a later section.

It is not only the professionals I've mentioned above who can find themselves in difficulty if information is not shared. You may remember back in 2016, Adam Johnson, Sunderland AFC player, was convicted on grooming and sexual activity with a child charges. Whilst the investigation was ongoing, Adam Johnson was allowed to continue to play for Sunderland AFC.

Initially, Sunderland AFC's view was that they'd done everything they possibly could and they released a statement saying that they did not know that he was going to plead guilty to the two charges and that he ultimately pled guilty on the first day of his trial. However, it came to light that the CEO of Sunderland knew that Adam Johnson admitted kissing the child, and that put a whole new spin on what Sunderland did and what they perhaps should have done in light of this knowledge.

Sharing information is something that we all need to do when we work with children where there are child protection concerns, but it is something that I think a lot of us are concerned to do. We worry about passing information on that perhaps we should not do, or that passing information on will cause problems for the people we are working with. We worry about the relationship we have with that person and how they will react.

Equally, there are often genuine concerns about the impact on us personally. What if you are wrong or the pattern of behaviour is nothing to worry about? Will the sharing of information do more harm than good?

Those are perfectly valid thoughts and worries. However, in a child protection situation, you need to think about what the ultimate outcome is going to be? Is this information that you hold going to be the information that is needed by another agency in order to protect the children? If the information is going to be needed by another agency, then very careful consideration needs to be given to what information is shared. Remember, child protection concerns trump data protection.

When a decision is made to share information, it should be done in a timely manner. There is nothing worse, in my professional opinion, than having information come through from a third party agency – perhaps a nursery or a GP – that says they had concerns about the parenting the child was receiving six months ago, or that the child was not getting nourishment or there were other issues. By the time that information was shared, it was too late to do anything urgently.

Sometimes information comes through and it is not recorded properly. I have seen recordings made on scrap paper. I'll be covering recording disclosures in a later section. Recordings are crucial information. Often it is the first time children's social care or the police are aware of the family or that incident. Make sure that anything that you have recorded is recorded properly. A formal document should be used. It could be a crucial document later down the line when children's social care or the police try and safeguard this child.

There are also new guidelines for sharing information.

The updated Keeping Children Safe in Education guidance, which came out in September 2016, gives a clear expectation of information being shared. There is a focus on making sure that children receive early help. That is, help given when concerns are first identified, and not several months, if not years, later when the situation becomes grave and, perhaps, unmanageable.

Whilst the focus of the guidance is on schools, the guidance is very useful for all agencies working with children. In relation to absences, schools are now obliged to tell their local authority of any pupil who does not attend regularly or who has been out of school for 10 consecutive school days without permission.

You can see that applying this to your own setting or organisation may be useful. You can monitor student's attendance for your own needs but, in doing so, if you notice there has been a significant period with no communication from them or the family you may consider contacting the school to see if the student has been attending, and to notify that they have not been seen by you. You may wish to by-pass the school and contact your local authority directly. Remember, they won't know about the absences as that is your piece of the jigsaw.

Information about a child can help determine whether or not a child is at risk of harm. It will also help determine what harm the child is at risk from. No piece of information should ever be seen as too small to share. That little piece of information could be the key piece which brings the other concerns together and frames the pieces to give clarity and understanding.

If you are worried about how to share information in your area, every authority and every area has a Local Safeguarding Children's Board (LSCB). That board will have policies and procedures about how information is to be shared appropriately. There will be multi-agency teams who will meet on a regular basis. Your organisation will be able to get in touch with the LSCB; their details will be on the internet.

If you have any concerns about sharing information, contact your Local Safeguarding Children's Board first. Do not sit on the information, thinking that you can't share it.

2 GETTING OVER THE NERVES

Sharing information and getting involved in the child protection process can be scary. This is especially true if you have never been involved before, or have only ever been on the edges.

Increasingly, professionals who are involved with children in the child protection arena are asked to get involved. That could be in writing reports, making a statement, or perhaps attending a conference or review meeting. In some circumstances you might even be asked to come to court. This can all be a bit terrifying.

One of my reasons for writing this book is to help you through the process. That not only includes what each stage is and how it can affect you; it also includes giving you some tried and tested tips on dealing with stressful situations. Those stressful situations will be different for everyone. Some people are fine recording a disclosure, others find that terrifying. Some are OK with attending a professionals meeting, others find the idea of just talking to a large group of adults makes them come out in a cold sweat. And I think most people find the idea of possibly having to go to court to give evidence absolutely petrifying.

In this section of the book I want to give you my top ten tips for dealing with difficult situations. I've been giving the same advice to social workers and teachers for years, and now I want to share it with you.

Tip one: Check your inner voice

We all have one. It is that annoying voice inside our heads that keeps on saying we can't do something, or won't be any good even if we try. It is a clever little voice, as it will change its tune depending on the circumstances. For many of us, our confidence disappears the moment we learn we have to attend a meeting, interview or review. That little voice starts to ask what they could want with us, and tells us that we don't know anything and that they won't take anything we have to say seriously.

Sometimes it comes out as a cold sweat, or we start to feel a little sick. And then the voice starts. Either way fear grips us and really does not want to let go.

For me, my inner voice starts to tell me I'm no good, I won't succeed at the task, so why even bother trying. Yours may say the same things or be even worse. Whatever it is saying to you, if you listen to it, you will never make progress.

It is not easy to ignore your inner voice. It has been with you since birth and has probably had a controlling vote on all of your decisions for time immemorial.

Now is the time for you to take charge.

It is not easy, and you will probably feel a bit daft talking to yourself, but it works. How many times have you seen films where a character is talking to themselves, psyching themselves up to do something. They're talking to their inner voice and an awful lot of people do it! Your inner voice will always talk and nag at you. How you react to it will determine how you handle the situation.

Be prepared for that voice to chat at you. Tell it to SHUT UP! Or ask it what it is worried about. I suspect it won't have an answer for you. You will be nervous, that's OK. Just don't let yourself be persuaded that you have nothing valid to say. You do, otherwise you wouldn't be there.

Tip two: Preparation

Ahead of any event, the key is preparation. It does not matter whether it is a meeting with parents or chairing a Multi-Agency Meeting.

As professionals we are all very busy. Trying to carve out more time to prepare for meetings or events in an already busy schedule can seem almost impossible. Trust me, giving yourself the time to prepare ahead can make a significant difference to how you feel about your situation.

Many professionals have mountains of information in their heads. Sometimes it can seem tempting to 'wing it', thinking that not worrying about the meeting will make you worry less. Whilst that may seem like a good strategy, it is often the cause of more stress and anxiety. In the meeting you will feel under-prepared and on the back foot. Sometimes vital information can be missed. As a consequence, your confidence wants to fly away. That all important sharing of information can be lost as you have not got the notes, or you have got so many notes you can't find the one you are looking for.

If you have to give a talk to a group of people, practice it beforehand. If you're chairing a meeting, make sure you have got everything you need before you begin. Do your homework and you will have any answers ready and be able to handle any questions thrown your way.

Tip three: Know where you are going

If the meeting is at a new venue or a room you have never been to before, try to visit it beforehand. A day or two before can be helpful so you know where you need to be. There's nothing worse for me than not knowing where I'm going. Almost inevitably, I get stuck in traffic or am delayed leaving. That makes me uncomfortable and practically guarantees I'm going to be late and possibly flustered. I don't like that feeling so I work out where I'm going. If I'm running late I try to call ahead.

If you can't check where you're going before and are worried about the layout, then try and check out the room before you go in. Learn where you will be standing or sitting and check any equipment you need is working. If you need to take notes, make sure you have a spare pen and plenty of paper. It is always at the most inconvenient of times that you run out or run late.

If you can't see the room – for example, if you are giving evidence in a court room – ask someone to explain the layout to you. Simply knowing what space you're walking into will help you keep a rein on your confidence.

Tip four: Know what you're trying to achieve

Many of us walk into meetings with no idea what it is for or what we want out of it. I've sat in many a meeting and had no clue what the other person wants from me. As a result they have gotten tongue-tied or had verbal diarrhoea. Neither is good when you're trying to hold onto your nerves.

Sometimes you will be called into a meeting or review at the last minute. Ask why you are needed. That way you can determine if you're the right person to go and what information you are going to need. It will give you some, if not a lot, of preparation time. If the person asking you to attend can't give you a reason why you have been asked to attend, then query why you are needed. You may be able to deal with the question over the phone or by email. It may be that you need to gather information before you go to the meeting in order to answer the query. Just because someone else does not know what they are looking to achieve, it does not mean you shouldn't.

Have an aim in a meeting, even if it is not your meeting. If you're meeting with parents, what is it you need to tell them, what information do you need from them? If you're chairing a meeting, what is the point of that meeting, what is its purpose? Know this and you will be better able to guide the meeting.

Where possible, have an agenda. For many meetings this will already be done and you should know what it is in advance. You will feel more confident in your own voice if you know where you're headed.

Tip five: Body language

One of the strongest actions you can take is to watch your body language. From that, your confidence will flow and nerves will slide away.

If you are really nervous, try some power poses. This may sound daft, and you will probably feel daft doing them to start with. These poses don't have to be obvious. A classic pose is to stand in a Wonder Woman pose: feet apart and hands on hips with head held high. An exaggerated pose will look unnatural, but simply standing taller in this pose will help. Do it in the car before you get out if you need to. Whilst you can't stand up, you can sit tall and straight, hold your head up and place your hand on your hips. No one need ever know what you were doing before you got out.

When you are in the meeting watch how you are sitting. When somebody's being aggressive or being very assertive, watch their body language. You will notice that they start to sit up straight, their shoulders are back, and their chest is out. You will see their chin is high and they are conveying that sense of power. They're conveying that sense of 'I'm in control here' and that can be a very tough thing to deal with if you're not used to it.

You can mirror their actions subtly. Be careful with this, depending on the person they can see this as a sign of aggression, and that's not what we want. Keeping your own body language in check is key. Watch how you're standing or sitting, watch where your arms are folded, are they folded in front of you, are they behind you? Are you sitting? Do you feel like you're crouching, or you're starting to fold in on yourself? If someone is being very assertive towards you and you need to deal with this, make sure you sit up straight, put both feet on the floor, uncross your arms, and keep your shoulders back and your head up. You are not looking to be aggressive but you are looking to be assertive. You are looking to say to the other person, "I have control of this situation and I'm going to manage it".

Your body language can, and should change, depending on the situation, As you get better at noticing your own language you will be better able to change your body language to suit the situation.

Tip six: Eye contact

Eye contact is a really powerful tool. I don't mean staring at the other person. You don't want to be trying to stare them down in a staring competition.

There's an awful lot you can get from eye contact. You can see whether there's anger or upset behind the eyes. You can see if someone's just tired and, as a result, they have come out with an inappropriate comment but they are absolutely shattered and not thinking straight. You can tell if they're sad, you can tell if there's something else going on there that they're not telling you and that can help you as you're dealing with the situation and the conflict further down the line.

Eye contact is a vital part of human contact. You can make

someone very comfortable, or uncomfortable, depending on the level of eye contact.

If you're in a meeting, eye contact with the person who asked the question can help you direct your response to them. If giving evidence, directing your answer to the Judge and catching their eye as you do so, will help make sure they hear your answer. Coupled with strong body language (standing tall etc.), eye contact can help you feel empowered and more in control.

Tip seven: Just breathe

It is really, really crucial to breathe. It is so easy not to breathe when you are feeling anxious. Often, when you have dealt with something, you realise that you have been holding your breath and you have not let that breath out.

Just breathe.

I know that is often easier said than done Sometimes you want to just get through your answer or the situation. As a result of panic or being uncomfortable, we forget to breathe normally.

Breathing will help calm you. Making sure you stop to pause for breathe will mean you don't rush or hurry through the situation. I find that if I'm in a difficult situation where I may have to give some difficult advice or I have to deal with a situation, like having to tell a Judge something that he really does not want to hear, that I breathe. This allows the body to just relax a bit.

It may take several breaths, but it does work.

Tip eight: Allow the silence

When you're sending breath to the right places, you are giving yourself a moment as well in that breath. You're letting yourself have that moment to essentially get ready and prepare for what you are about to say and what you are about to do.

When you're feeling under pressure it can be really easy to want to fill those silent moments and not allow that breath.

Don't.

Use them to your advantage. Give yourself the time to think, re-group and consider your next comments. This can be essential if you are giving evidence. It can also really help in a meeting with parents or your peers. That moment of silence will let you gather your thoughts, quickly reflect on what has just been said and think about where the meeting needs to go next.

Tip nine: Clear distractions

It is all too easy to have multiple distractions. Sometimes that might be a child who is demanding your attention when you need to have a difficult conversation. Often it is a mobile phone which may be out. Maybe it is a TV on in the background, or another auditory device.

All these things take away from your ability to control the situation and, as such, you may find yourself trying to deal with several things at once. That does your confidence or nerves no good.

Ask for devices to be put down and TVs turned off. If you're in a meeting, make sure phones are away and that there will be no interruptions. Knowing there will be no distractions means you can say what you need to sooner and that you have better control of the situation.

Simply remembering your body language and to breathe will help you immediately if the situation demands it.

3 WHERE ARE WE HEADED?

Before we go in to the steps that form the child protection process, I thought it would be helpful to share where the whole process heads.

In many cases intervention, early help and support means that the child protection process stops before any court proceedings are considered. However, in ever increasing cases, court proceedings are exactly where families and professionals find themselves.

As we will discuss in later sections, a local authority has a duty to children in their area to promote their welfare needs. If, in spite of significant support and guidance, families cannot do this, then a local authority will look to the court arena to protect children. They will also look that way when a child has suffered a serious non-accidental injury or when it would be a danger to a child's welfare for them to return home.

A local authority may ask parents, or those with parental responsibility, to voluntary accommodate their children in foster care whilst investigations are ongoing. This is not a long term solution and should last no longer than three months, generally speaking. It also requires the agreement of everyone with parental responsibility. A social worker cannot rely on only one person with parental responsibility agreeing to this. There are rules around children going into care on a voluntary basis, which are outside the scope of this book.

Let's work on the basis that all other interventions have been tried and there is still a risk to the child. What happens then?

Essentially, a social worker will contact their in-house legal team to find out if they have enough evidence to go to court. This is called the threshold for proceedings. The threshold is set out in s31(2) Children Act 1989. It says:

(2) A court may only make a care order or supervision order if it is satisfied—
(a) that the child concerned is suffering, or is likely to suffer, significant harm; and
(b) that the harm, or likelihood of harm, is attributable to—
(i) the care given to the child, or likely to be given to him if the order were not made, not being what it would be reasonable to expect a parent to give to him; or
(ii) the child's being beyond parental control.

If the decision is that the threshold criteria has been met, as above, then the local authority will look to go to court for a court order. That order could be to share parental responsibility (a care order) and give the local authority more say in a child's life than the parents. The order could also be to befriend and assist the child (a supervision order). There could also be no order, sometimes used when legal judgements need to be made but no order is necessary.

Whatever the reason, it is a very serious step.

You might find it useful to look at the flow chart which sets out the steps to be taken in care proceedings. You can find that at www.kateyoung.org/documents.

The flow chart starts with the initial referral and goes all the way through to the end of court proceedings.

There is a strict timescale of 26 weeks for any court proceedings. The court's aim is to make sure decisions are made about a child's long term future as soon as possible. There is little time for further evidence gathering, the expectation being that a local authority will have gathered all its evidence before starting proceedings.

I want to pause here for a moment before we look at the time scales and the impact on you. There are three points I want you to remember:

1. Whilst it is hoped a child can remain living within their birth family, one possible outcome for the child is living away from their birth family permanently. That could be through adoption or long term foster care.

2. The information you provide during the child protection process can influence the local authority's long term plans for a child.

3. Knowing point one should never prevent you from sharing information and taking part in supporting the family during the process.

Timescales and impact

Not that long ago, cases involving children and local authorities could take upwards of 12 months and, in rare cases, up to three years. Clearly that's not in a child's best interests. Rule number one when dealing with children's cases is that the child's welfare is of paramount consideration. It is all about the child.

As a result, the most senior family judge, Mr. Justice Munby, stated that this all needed to change.

Historically, there was heavy use of expert evidence and the child was getting lost in the proceedings. The Family Court decided that this could not happen anymore.

A local authority has to prove a child is at risk of significant harm and it has to prove that on the balance of probabilities. So part of the local authority's case is all about gathering evidence in order to demonstrate to the court and prove to the court that a child is at risk of significant harm. It does that by undertaking assessments. At the initial referral stage, there is an initial investigation and at the next stage, and throughout, a local authority is continually assessing how parents are engaging, and if they are co-operating with the agencies they have signed up to work with as part of these agreements with the local authority.

The evidence will look at whether they are attending meetings and parenting courses, and this information forms the local authority's case. The basis for the local authority's case includes information from police, health, medical assessments and so on (this is not an exhaustive list). Therefore, if there have been missed appointments or they are continually missing appointments for the child or children, then the local authority will potentially want to receive reports from the GP, the hospital where the appointments are being missed, or the consultant to find out what the concerns are there and what the potential impact is on a child if they're missing these appointments.

There is an onus on you to make sure you keep the social worker informed about engagement, attendance and presentation. That can be for both the children and the parents. You hold that part of the jigsaw.

The local authority will also consider any family members that may be able to provide care for these children, in addition to assessing parents to find out whether they are engaging and how they are working with professionals. They may do a parenting assessment with the parents or carers and go through the basics in terms of how and what a child needs in order to have its basic needs met.

A local authority works on a case by case basis, so I'm talking very generally here and every case will have different nuances in it. However, you need to be aware as a professional involved on the periphery of care proceedings, that if parents are not turning up for appointments with you, the local authority is going to want to know about that.

For example, you should share information if:

- A child turns up late on a very regular basis.
- There are problems in terms of their presentation.
- They are turning up to nursery in grubby clothes, unwashed, and not having been fed.
- They are not turning up to appointments that you have scheduled. If you work in health, or are a drug worker, are parents turning up and being tested?

All of this information is gathered at the pre-proceedings stage but the information above can be useful if it is updated throughout the proceedings, especially in relation to drugs and engagement.

The courts will not tolerate cases taking 12 months plus, children being lost in the process, and children's needs not being met as quickly as possible. The courts decided that all the assessments that we will look at need to happen at the beginning. They are going to have to be updated as they go through, because we need to get these cases finished for children much more quickly. This is how the 26 week time scale came into being. It has been in place since July 2013 and came into law in April 2014.

4 DISCLOSURES AND REFERRALS

Being told something concerning by a child can happen to any professional working with them. There are lots and lots of texts and guides dealing solely with this issue. This section is not the definitive text on dealing with disclosures, but rather a guide to help you navigate your way when a disclosure is made to you.

I have seen too many bad examples of recordings being made. Professionals who should know better but yet get caught out. Professionals who break the basic rules as they think they are doing the best thing. This is the area in which most people get caught out.

If you work with children you're going to have a disclosure made at some point, and it is really important that you get this down correctly. It records the nature of the disclosure for the professionals further up the child protection process chain. It is a contemporary note of what was said to you by the child in question. However, given it is such a crucial document I see time and again disclosure forms that are done on scraps of paper, that don't give the full information and actually lead to more questions being asked than answers given.

In this context, a disclosure is anything said by a child which alerts you to a child protection concern. It may be about the child themselves or about another child. Sometimes the child will not know the significance of what they have said. They may not understand that what is happening is abuse or that they are being abused. In some circumstances the report of abuse can come years after it has taken place or after they have left your organisation or setting.

There are some very basic rules to follow when a disclosure of abuse is made. The disclosure may come about as you have noticed something unusual on a child, such as a bruise, or have seen an injury a parent has not mentioned. You may need to check if there is a child protection concern. Sometimes it is not obvious. In that situation you should use open questions to gently find out if there is a child protection issue. Once it is established whether or not there is a child protection issue, you stop asking questions. The biggest thing to remember is you are not investigating. That is not your role in this context.

Disclosures happen when you are least expecting it. You must remember to remain calm and not appear shocked at what you are being told. Be sympathetic to the victim; listen carefully to what is being said as you will need to make a full note of it. Depending on the disclosure, medical evidence may be needed.

You should tell the person they have done the right thing in telling you what is going on and that you are treating it seriously. They may want you to keep the information secret. You cannot do this and should not promise to do so. Instead tell them you what you will be doing with the information. Your setting or organisation should have a child protection policy setting this out.

As I said above, in order to accurately record what has been said, you will need to listen. Most of us are not very good when it comes to really hearing what someone is truly saying.

If possible, keep distractions to a minimum during the conversation. This can be difficult if you are in the playground or classroom. If other students try to interrupt, this can deter the victim from proceeding.

During any conversation your internal monologue will want to weigh in. It is tricky to turn off your own voice; however, if you really want to listen you will need to keep checks on your inner voice. You may need to teach yourself to focus. You should not make judgements or interrupt them with your own stories.

Using good eye contact shows the victim they have your attention and that you're ready to listen. Maintain eye contact rather than looking everywhere else. The nature of the disclosure can make you feel very uncomfortable. If the victim feels you are uncomfortable, they may be unwilling to tell you the whole issue.

Also, be aware that some people find eye contact off-putting. It does, however, usually help with empathy. If the child is younger, then getting to their level can help too.

You may also have a number of questions you really want to ask. It can be very easy to jump into the conversation with your own comments. Don't do it, however strong the urge. By all means use encouraging comments, gestures or noises to allow the other person to continue. Such motions will help you to get the whole story from the other person.

Also be aware that any closed questions (those that prompt yes or no answers) can be seen as directing the conversation and could jeopardise any investigation. Remember it is not your role to investigate. You are to listen, encourage, support and, importantly, accurately record what is said.

The point of the conversation is to allow the other person to tell you what is on their mind. You want to let the conversation flow. Let the person reach the end of their story in their own time. It can be easy to allow yourself to try and steer the conversation to get information *you* think is necessary. You may want to probe deeper and dig to find out more information. In doing so you may miss something important you were not aware of previously. Again, trying to direct the conversation can jeopardise any future investigation. Be very careful not to do this.

The victim may need time to think about what they want to say next. Even children and young people need time to put their thoughts in order. Be empathetic. For example, you may say "I can see you are upset". This will encourage the victim to keep sharing.

You may be asked for a solution. It is highly unlikely you will have one, and it is unlikely to be your role to provide one. It is important to tell the victim what is going to happen next. Be careful not to judge in your response and always be respectful, regardless of what you actually think.

We talked earlier about body language. It is just as important here. If the information is uncomfortable to hear, you may react with closed body language. Try to stay open. Watch for your arms folding or your torso curling up.

After the disclosure has been made it is time to record it. It is really crucial that you record what was said as soon as possible, and make appropriate referrals swiftly. Sometimes a referral does not have to be made. This is a decision which will be made by your safeguarding lead. Where possible, when a referral has to be made, consent of the family should be obtained. If this is not forthcoming it should not prevent you from making the referral, and the wishes should be made clear when the referral is made. Sometimes consent should not be sought before a referral is made. For example, where a child is injured or where disclosing the comments to the family could place the child at risk of significant harm. Again, this is not definitive and you should discuss all situations with your safeguarding lead.

As part of your recording you need to say what was said, what happened, and what was going on at the time the disclosure was made. It can also be helpful to make a note of what was going on when the disclosure was made. You should use the victims own words and phrasing.

You should also record where the alleged abuse took place, if that has been disclosed. For example, was it on a school trip? Did it take place in a person's home or was it in a public place? Also record where you were when the child made the disclosure to you. Where were you at the time that this came out? Were you on a school trip? Were you in the playground with the child? Was it something that you were talking about in the classroom that triggered this disclosure, potentially? Maybe you'd finished practice or the child was the only person left after an activity? Be very clear on where things happened.

Also consider using a body map to record where bruises or other injuries appeared on a child.

Note when the thing that the child is making the disclosure about happened. Was it day time? Was it night time? Does the child have any idea when it was? Are we talking recently, as in the last couple of days or the last couple of weeks, or are we talking a bit longer than that? Are we talking about months ago? Are we talking about something that happened in the summer holidays or on a weekend with a particular parent or carer? Get all the detail down in your record of the disclosure.

Also, consider when the disclosure was made in the school day. Was it at playtime, dinnertime, first thing in the morning, at an after school club?

Who is the child referring to as the person that's done this particular thing? Who else was around at the time? Was the child on their own with this particular person? Was the child with somebody else when this happened? Were there a few people around? Were there other adults around at the time? If so, who were they? Does the child know them? Who did they tell? Did they tell anybody else other than you? Did they say anything to their parents or to their carers? What about brothers and sisters that were around? Did they say anything else to another member of staff? Is this how you have become involved?

Remember to not probe for the answers to these questions. They are here as a guide to the sort of things you should record if disclosed. This is not an exhaustive list in any way.

You may want to consider who else was around when this disclosure was made to you. If you were in the playground, were there other pupils around with you or was the child on their own? Was there another teacher present, or has the child come up to you on their own as well?

Get all information down on a proper disclosure form, not a piece of paper torn out of a book or been lying around in the classroom or on your desk. You should have a proper disclosure form for this.

Having all that information on the record of disclosure means you are making a proper and factual full note of what has gone on. This will help the professionals coming in after you, depending on the nature of the disclosure, such as social workers, GPs or other professionals, to have a full idea of what was happening.

If the disclosure results in court proceedings (either criminal or removing the child from the family), your record of the disclosure could be crucial. It may be the only solid piece of evidence available to help protect the child.

Make sure your record of the disclosure is professional. Once completed, sign and date it, and keep it together with any body maps you have used.

Reporting the disclosure

You should never ignore a disclosure, however insignificant it may seem to you. Your organisation will have a process for sharing that information. As a minimum, where the disclosure is one of harm by a person outside your setting, you need to report it to the safeguarding lead. They will then determine what happens next.

Do not share the disclosure with colleagues unless advised to do so.

Refer

It is usually the role of the safeguarding lead to decide what happens next. Is that something that happens immediately? Is it something that needs to be referred on? Or is it something that is actually low level and can be considered at a later stage? If it is the latter one, keep a record of the disclosure in a safe place, following the policies and procedures, and know what you need to do with it.

Keep an eye on the situation, don't forget about it. Keep a regular check on disclosures that come up.

If it is a referral that needs to be made, is it immediate? Is there an immediate risk of harm to this child or children? Ask yourself 'Do I need to act now?' If so, ring the police, ring the local authority, and do not delay. If not, make the referral when you need to. Make it in a timely manner and the local authority will take over their steps as appropriate or the police will act as they see fit.

Key points

- Keep calm when a disclosure is being made.
- Do not investigate.
- Record everything accurately, using the victim's words and phrases.
- Be professional in your recording.

- Do not ignore it.
- Share with your safeguarding lead.
- Check if you need to refer immediately.
- Make any referrals in a timely manner.

5 STRATEGY MEETINGS

A strategy meeting is a meeting which takes place between professionals when there has been an assessment that a child is at risk of suffering significant harm. The meeting decides whether or not there is sufficient evidence and sufficient grounds for the matter to proceed to a Section 47 Enquiry. The meeting will determine the next steps to be taken by each of the professional bodies, and the time frames in which these enquiries will be completed.

A strategy meeting is called by either the police or children's social care. It follows the assessment that a child is at risk of significant harm. That assessment can be completed by the police, a health professional, or children's social care. Occasionally, other agencies will make an assessment but it usually those three agencies that will make the call that a child is at risk of significant harm.

You may know strategy meetings as being more common where there has been an injury to a child. Such an injury could be bruising or a bone breakage. The child is usually taken to a GP or the hospital where these injuries are noted, and the treating medic makes an assessment that the injuries to the child are non-accidental. Alternatively, the medic may find the parents' explanation for how the injuries were caused does not account fully or at all for how the injuries have come to be.

When such a call is made, each health authority has its own specific procedures to follow which are in line with child protection policies and procedures. In general terms, the medic will contact the named person within children's social care and/or the police at the same time. Sometimes children's social care contacts the police on behalf of the child. Again, this can depend on the severity.

The strategy meeting can be crucial to how a child protection investigation continues. It is the first opportunity for professionals to get together and discuss the concerns that each of them have.

A strategy meeting has to be called within X number of days, and can be held in a variety of places. Strategy meetings have been held in hospitals, police stations, schools, and children's services departments. It is important that the meeting is arranged with as many professionals able to attend as possible. The person who has made the assessment should be in attendance as their evidence can be crucial as to what next steps need to be taken.

In general terms, the following people should be in attendance:

- Children's social worker
- Children's social work team manager
- Treating medic and/or GP
- Health visitor
- Child protection police officer
- Safeguarding lead for the nursery or school
- Teacher or head teacher (including nursery managers)

The meeting is usually headed by the children's social work team manager. It is children's social care who will be taking the lead on any Section 47 investigation, should that be necessary. Minutes must be taken at strategy meetings. These can become required at a later date, in the event that care proceedings are taken.

The Chair of the meeting (children's social work manager) will outline the reasons why the strategy meeting has been called and what the concerns are. If possible, there should be a chronology of events to assist people. Each person attending should provide a written report of their concerns. If the meeting has been called because of a medical reason, the medic's child protection report should be shared with all persons present. That report is confidential and should not be shared outside of the meeting.

The meeting then proceeds with all those present introducing themselves so the minutes can have an accurate record.

The meeting should then turn to whoever made the assessment that a child was at risk of significant harm. That person will then outline how they reached that assessment. They will set out the steps they took, the examinations they made, and any discussions they had with parents which have led to the decision that a child is at risk of significant harm.

Once the person who has made the assessment has finished outlining their position and how they reached their conclusions, the Chair will move around the room asking each person present in turn for their report and any views that they have.

Health

Depending on the child's age, the health visitor or GP can be asked whether or not, in the event the issue is an injury, whether such injuries have taken place previously or whether the child has been a regular attender at the surgery and if any other concerns have been raised prior to this incident taking place. The purpose for this is to allow the Chair to have a full view of what is happening in that child's life. A history of missed appointments can lead a children's services department to think about matters in one particular direction. However, a history of children being taken to the GP for a variety of minor complaints and/or issues which cannot be determined, may lead the children's services department to consider whether or not there is something else taking place (such as fabricated illnesses).

Education

In terms of education, the professionals at the meeting will want to know whether the child is a regular attender at nursery or school, what their pattern of attendance is like, whether there are any concerns around presentation or parents' behaviour, and whether there have been incidents occurring in the playground previously which, depending on the circumstances, could give some background to the injury or situation currently being discussed by the panel. The Chair is looking at building up a picture of this child's life. Whether something is normal or not for a particular child can be pivotal in how a matter is dealt with and indicative of a child's home life. It will help the social worker to consider how best to proceed and what steps need to be taken in order to protect the child's welfare in the future.

If the teacher is not able to attend, it is important that whoever attends has a knowledge of the child and is able to provide information to the meeting about that child's life in school. This can include any meetings they have had with parents, how parents present at school, as well as any issues with siblings or other caregivers. If there are any records within the school of incidents, these should be made known to the meeting. The meeting will ask for a short report around the child. Attendance records are very useful. Given the nature of strategy meetings, and the speed with which they need to be arranged, it can be very difficult to have a full report prepared in time. The importance of an attendance record shouldn't be overlooked. Whilst they can be provided and handed out, it is important that the analysis of it is provided by the teacher or head teacher so that the panel has a full understanding of what is going on. Whilst I appreciate attendance records can be very easy to read at a glance if you look at them every day, it can be very hard for those who only see them periodically to understand whether there is a pattern emerging or not, in terms of a child's attendance, late record, or absence.

Police

The police have a very important role next to children's social care. It will be the police that take any criminal investigation on. They will be attending the meeting to consider whether or not they are able to look at a prosecution. The police will also be able to provide to the panel any criminal records of the parents or caregivers. The police involvement can be really important when you are looking at a new partner who is not the child's biological parent. The police record of that person may be completely unknown to the parent. Statistically, a child who is abused is more likely to have been abused by a member of their own family rather than a stranger. As such, knowing the background to a caregiver can be crucial when looking at whether or not that person poses a risk to a child.

Once everybody at the meeting has set out their position, a discussion will then follow about how best to proceed. Depending on the severity of the case, it may be that the police request that no action is taken and parents are not spoken to any further until they have been arrested and interviewed. This is to preserve evidence and to ensure, as far as possible, that the criminal investigation is not compromised. The police may also request that there is an Achieving Best Evidence interview of the child or children. Depending on the circumstances, this may have already taken place or may need to be arranged following the strategy meeting. Depending on the circumstances, the police may take the view that they need to exercise emergency powers and remove the children from the parents' care immediately. This is commonly known as a Police Protection Order, but no such order actually exists. Rather, it is the police exercising their powers to safeguard the children from a dangerous situation.

The point of the discussion is, as I say, to determine the next step. If the police are going to pursue a criminal investigation, and interview the children and parents, it is likely that the social worker will want to have that information before it proceeds and before they conclude the Section 47 Enquiry. This can sometimes be difficult, given the time constraints on a Section 47 Enquiry. Sometimes the police are unable to interview parents within that time frame. This can happen for a variety of reasons but can be a problem which the social worker will have to overcome as part of their assessment.

The purpose of the meeting is to:

1. Ensure information is shared among the relevant agencies.

2. Agree whether or not a criminal investigation is necessary, and the timing of that.

3. Agree whether or not a Section 47 Enquiry should be instigated by the local authority.

4. Determine how the Section 47 investigation should be carried out. This is to ensure that the investigation can be completed in a timely fashion with the relevant medical evidence and police information.

5. Decide whether there should be any immediate protective measures in place.

6. Decide what information, if any, should be shared with the family and/or other caregivers.

7. Determine what, if any, legal action needs to be taken in order to protect the child.

If this is your first strategy meeting, you may be anxious about what will be asked of you and what information you will need to have with you. The explanation above will give you guidance on those particular issues. Whatever agency you work for, you will need to have the relevant information for that particular child.

Remember also that the decision does not rest on your shoulders. The purpose of the strategy meeting is to determine the steps to be taken as set out above. That is a collective decision. The decision about criminal proceedings is taken by the police, and the decision about Section 47 Enquiries will be taken by the social work manager. That said, the decisions are made following the information given by the members of the strategy meeting. As a result, it is very important that all relevant information is shared. If you are unsure about whether or not something is relevant, then ask. The members of the meeting will soon inform you whether it is something that is pertinent to the enquiry or not. Remember also that they will not have all the same information that you have. Each member of the meeting holds a different piece of the jigsaw. The purpose of the meeting is to put all those pieces of the jigsaw together. The missing pieces of the jigsaw are the elements of work that need to be completed in order to safeguard the child, such as a police investigation, a further medical investigation to determine some other elements, and the Section 47 Enquiry to look at the situation as a whole. Your role within the meeting is to provide your piece of the jigsaw to the rest of the group. Without your piece of the jigsaw the picture will never be complete.

Key points

- Strategy meetings are held to determine the next steps of an investigation.

- They are a forum for professionals to discuss concerns and decide how to proceed.
- Bring as much information with you as possible.

- Be prepared to be part of the ongoing investigation.
- Have a view.

6 INITIAL ENQUIRIES / SECTION 47 ENQUIRIES

Section 47 of The Children Act places a legal duty on local authorities to make enquiries into the circumstances of the children who are the subject of the enquiry.

S47(1) Children Act 1989 says:

(1) Where a local authority—

(a) are informed that a child who lives, or is found, in their area—
(i) is the subject of an emergency protection order; or
(ii) is in police protection;
(b) have reasonable cause to suspect that a child who lives, or is found, in their area is suffering, or is likely to suffer, significant harm, the authority shall make, or cause to be made, such enquiries as they consider necessary to enable them to decide whether they should take any action to safeguard or promote the child's welfare.

These are children who are deemed to be at risk of significant harm. The local authority is under a duty to investigate these referrals and, if necessary, to dictate what action is needed in order to safeguard and promote the child or children's welfare.

When you have made your referral, the next step is for a local authority to consider how to proceed with the referral that has been made. The process that is followed is known as the Initial Enquiries, or Section 47 Enquiries.

They are known as Section 47 Enquiries because it is Section 47 of The Children Act 1989 which sets out the process the local authority has to follow when referrals are made. The extract above is only a small section from that particular section of the Act. There are 12 different sections to s47 telling the local authority what its responsibilities are.

The investigation itself forms part of the local authority's core assessment. This is also known as a single or initial assessment, or a social work analysis of needs. Every area seems to have a different name for this initial assessment but its purpose is the same.

The assessment looks at the child's needs and also the ability of his or her parents or carers to meet those needs. It will consider the wider family, including grandparents, aunts and uncles on both maternal and paternal sides of the family. It will also consider any community involvement with the child, such as playgroups, school and youth groups, for example.

This initial assessment will form the basis of the evidence the local authority has, should it decide to take court proceedings in respect of the children and apply to the court for either a Care Order or a Supervision Order.

The local authority's duty under Section 47 of The Children Act arises where:

- The local authority already has an Emergency Protection Order in relation to the child; or,

- Where the local authority is told by way of referral that there is a child in its area who is the subject of a Child Emergency Protection Order where the police have exercised that powers of police protection where a child has contravened a ban imposed by a curfew Notice under Section 14 of the Crime and Disorder Act 1998 and the local authority has reasonable cause to suspect that a child in its area is suffering, or is likely to suffer, significant harm.

The purpose of the Section 47 enquiry is to find out whether or not it is necessary to take any action to safeguard or promote the child's welfare as well as what that action should be.

If the police have exercised their powers of protection, then a Strategy meeting will be convened (see later chapter).

It is always the responsibility of the local authority where the child lives to undertake the Section 47 enquiry. Sometimes this can be the subject of much discussion where a child is found in another area but is not technically living in that area. In those circumstances, the local authority must tell the local authority where the child normally lives and that home local authority should be involved in future strategy discussions and meetings, and can often be asked to assist in the enquiries that need to be made with the parents, family and wider community.

The Children Act places a duty on all professionals within health, education and other services to assist the local authority when they are making their initial enquiries. All agencies have a duty to inform the local authority of any information they hold in respect of the child or children, and they have a duty to assist the local authority with the Section 47 Enquiries.

Not every referral will result in a Section 47 Enquiry being made. However, an assessment is likely to be undertaken if one of the following apply:

- Allegation of sexual abuse
- Any injury, however minor, to a non-mobile infant or child
- Serious physical injury, either alleged or suspected
- A repeat non-accidental injury
- Neglect
- Repeat neglect
- Deliberate harm being caused to a child
- No consistent explanation for injuries or abuse caused

- Reasonable cause to suspect the child is likely to suffer, or is suffering, significant harm in the form of either physical, sexual or emotional abuse or neglect
- Where there has been domestic violence between carers and the child has been injured, even if inadvertently.

As stated above, there is a duty on all professionals under The Children Act to assist the local authority in the making of Section 47 enquiries. However, the local authority will take the lead within the investigation. The police will be responsible for undertaking any criminal investigation.

It can be easy to think that once a referral has been made, there is little for a third party agency to do. The Section 47 investigations can, and should be, in-depth. They require a great deal of information being provided to them from third parties. As someone who works with the child, you may find that you are being asked an awful lot of questions and an awful lot of documentation is being requested of you.

Every case is different. Every case will need to have sufficient evidence gathered in order for the local authority to decide and to determine the next stages and steps to be taken. The information requested of you can vary from case to case. There are often, however, a number of documents that are the same for nearly every investigation that takes place. This information may be different depending on the agency you work for, but it is a useful starting point when Section 47 enquiries are undertaken.

Health

If you are a Health Visitor then it is highly likely that your notes and any records you have made will be required by the local authority. The local authority will want to see what work has been done with the family. In some cases, parents will state that they were simply following the advice of the Health

Visitor. In order to corroborate this information and the parents' position, the local authority will want to see the details of the Health Visitor involvement. It also helps the local authority to establish whether or not there has been a pattern of behaviour or incidents. Sometimes children can be presented to clinics or health surgeries on a frequent basis. Sometimes key appointments are missed which tally up with dates when alleged injuries or abuse have allegedly taken place.

Any reports that are provided to the local authority at this stage may well be used by local authorities in court proceedings, should they become necessary at a later date. It is therefore very important that these reports are written properly and within the correct format.

Education

If the child is at nursery, a report from the Nursery Manager or Key Worker may be requested. It would be very helpful for a local authority for the report to set out the attendance of the child, to confirm whether or not it is regular and on time. I know it has become practice due to very busy workloads and schedules for attendance records simply to be appended to short reports prepared by nursery staff. Interpreting attendance records can be something of an art form and not always the most helpful document to have.

Any information you have about any discussions with parents around the concerns that have caused the enquiry to be made should also be passed to the local authority. Sometimes the information that nurseries or educational establishments hold can help form a good picture of what life is like for the children. For example, if parents are not disclosing that injuries have taken place and you are discovering them in the setting, you may a number of records within your setting which haven't led to a referral until perhaps the third or fourth injury. All of those records will be pertinent to the local authority's investigation and will assist the local authority in determining what assistance may be required in order to promote and protect the child's welfare.

For primary school children, their attendance records and a report from their teacher is often required. Details on their attendance, attainment, punctuality and presentation are often key to helping form that picture of a family. This is particularly the case where a family is not known to a local authority prior to the referral being made.

For secondary school children, the information required within the report to the local authority is much the same as for primary school children. It can often be helpful as well as to include details of their friendship groups, whether they are attending class on time, their abilities within class, and any concerns you may have about their associates and friends within school.

For those working in education, it can be very helpful for a local authority, and later a court, for you to paint a picture of what life is actually like for that child or children within your setting. Are they attending on time? Who brings them in? Who takes them home? Are there are issues with them being fed? Are they hungry when they turn up? Are they dirty? Do they have the appropriate clothing? Who are their friends? Do these raise any questions, queries or concerns for you? If so, tell the local authority why they raise concerns.

You see these children on a daily basis. You are in a prime position to advise and inform a local authority about the children's day-to-day life and their needs. Clear, factually-based recordings and descriptions of a child's life can significantly improve the ability of a local authority to ensure a child's needs are met and promote his or her welfare. This is because they have a very clear view, right from the beginning, of what that child's life is like. They can assist schools and the family to meet the needs of the child or children by putting in appropriate support and funding, if necessary at an early stage.

Police

I said above that the police are responsible for the criminal investigation. It is important to remember that a criminal investigation or further police involvement is not always required. Indeed, in many cases, a police investigation is never carried out.

The Group Manager within Children's Social Care has the responsibility to be the lead liaison with the police if there is an investigation. In some circumstances, the police may request that a Section 47 enquiry is delayed. This may be to preserve evidence, to allow them time to question alleged perpetrators who may be parents or carers of the child, or to prevent information being shared with the parents or carers that they think would compromise the police investigation.

It is the Group Manager of the Children's Social Care team who has responsibility for making the decision as to whether or not a Section 47 enquiry is undertaken. They do so based upon the information shared by the police, and by considering the risk posed to the child or children.

In coming to this decision, the Manager must look at:

- The seriousness of the concerns.
- Whether this is a repetition of alleged abuse, and/or the duration of the concerns.
- The vulnerability of the child or children. This could be through their age, development or any other factor.
- Where the concerns have come from, such as who has made the referral.
- Whether there is enough information in order to proceed.
- The situation in which the child is living.

- Whether there are any other factors which make this child at higher risk or the case a higher risk, such as substance misuse, history of domestic violence or mental health concerns.

Whilst the police may have concerns about the impact on their own investigation, it is important to note that a Section 47 enquiry must commence immediately where there are concerns that a child is suffering or is likely to suffer significant harm.

When a referral is made, the Children's Social Care Manager must inform the police at the earliest possible opportunity. The local authority and police should consult with each other, including the Police Child Abuse Investigation Unit and any other agencies which may be involved with the family.

Should a crime be suspected, then there should be no delay in informing the police of this.

In conducting their enquiries, the police should continue to share information with the local authority about their findings and other agencies involved with the family. The sharing of information jointly allows all the agencies to consider the best course of action in order to protect the children.

The local authority must, within one working day, make a police referral wherever there's an allegation of abuse being made that may also be an allegation of a crime taking place. The Police Child Abuse Investigation Unit Manager will then determine whether to investigate once initial checks have been made.

In terms of sharing information with a local authority for Section 47 enquiries, in the event there is no child protection criminal investigation, the information often required is that of police records. This is not simply the criminal records of carers or parents. It includes any police logs in respect of domestic abuse, callouts to the family home, callouts in relation to any of the carers, and callouts in relation to any of the children.

Pocket book note entries are also useful and may be requested in addition to the other police checks mentioned above.

In all of these cases it is important to remember that every area will have its own miniature protocol as to what is expected of each agency. Some areas will provide detailed guidance through your local Safeguarding Children's Board. Some areas will have agreements that are done by way of historic workings. If you are in doubt as to any of the information you need to provide, the purpose of this book is to give you an idea of what is required. If anything in addition to this is required, then it is helpful to find out from your Line Manager and to make a note of it, particularly if this is something you're going to be required to provide on a regular basis.

Key points

- This is an evidence gathering process.
- The outcome of the assessment determines what, if anything, needs to happen next.
- You may be asked to provide information as part of the assessment – do so in a timely manner.
- Any new information about the family should be shared.
- Make yourself aware of your local practices for initial assessments.

7 CHILD IN NEED PROCESS

Every local authority has its own Child in Need process and procedures. Each of these procedures is backed up by the policies and procedures of the local Safeguarding Children Board.

The Child in Need process stems from Section 17 of the Children Act 1989. S17(1) states that:

(1) It shall be the general duty of every local authority (in addition to the other duties imposed on them by this Part)—

(a) to safeguard and promote the welfare of children within their area who are in need; and
(b) so far as is consistent with that duty, to promote the upbringing of such children by their families,
by providing a range and level of services appropriate to those children's needs.

S17 is a much larger section than this paragraph. It sets out the role the local authority has and it is duties.

The purpose of the Child in Need process is to ensure that every child in a local authority's area has his or her welfare needs met. It ensures that professionals work together to make sure that these needs are being met and that all agencies are sharing information so that that particular child's jigsaw can be as complete as possible.

S17(10) of the Children Act 1989 sets out the definition of a child in need:

10) For the purposes of this Part a child shall be taken to be in need if—

(a) he is unlikely to achieve or maintain, or to have the opportunity of achieving or maintaining, a reasonable standard of health or development without the provision for him of services by a local authority under this Part;
(b) his health or development is likely to be significantly impaired, or further impaired, without the provision for him of such services; or
(c) he is disabled,
and "family", in relation to such a child, includes any person who has parental responsibility for the child and any other person with whom he has been living.

A local authority can fulfil its duties in a number of ways:

- By providing money.
- By providing items of clothing.
- By providing items of furniture.
- Assisting the family in removing rubbish and clutter from the home and garden.
- Assisting with transportation.
- Assisting with practical items.

This list is not exhaustive. A local authority can fulfil its duties under Section 17 in a wide variety of ways. Money provided may be for taxis or bus fare to various appointments or meetings. It can include transport to and from school for children. It can also include local authorities paying rent for a family if they are unable to earn or claim benefits by virtue of their immigration status.

A local authority will also look to other agencies that may be able to assist a family. There are a number of charities in every area who are able to provide assistance on a range of issues. Some charities and organisations will assist in helping families clear and redecorate properties and gardens. Others will assist by providing essential items, from white goods to food parcels.

Increasingly, due to budget constraints, local authorities are looking to other agencies to assist. Sometimes other agencies are able to help families in a way that local authorities can't simply because, for some families, having the stigma of a local authority being involved with them can mean that they are reluctant to engage in the services that they so desperately need. By having other agencies involved, some of whom they may have been involved with previously, and who are not directly connected to the local authority, can make the assistance easier to accept and ensure that a child or children's welfare needs are being met.

The Child in Need process does not stand alone. It follows on from initial enquiries being made by a local authority, the conclusion of those enquiries being that the family does not need the significant involvement of a child protection process, but that there is sufficient concern to prevent the local authority from moving out of the family's lives.

It is important to remember that any child in any area can become a child in need. The economic difficulties which have led to funding being removed or significantly cut has had a huge impact on middle income as well as low income families. Many of the services – such as those in Surestart centres, parents groups, parenting courses, groups for dads, domestic abuse victim and perpetrator courses, not to mention the individual support team that local authorities would have in family support workers – have either disappeared altogether or been depleted significantly. As a result, families who were previously able to manage with some support from the local authority or support groups, have found themselves in positions whereby this support has disappeared or, as a result of a growing need, they are not seen as needing as much support initially. Sadly, this often leads to a situation whereby those families who were just about getting by are finding life ever-difficult, and their children become children in need by virtue of the depleted services available.

It is important to remember that whilst most of the cases on a local authority's caseload do involve children from lower income families, there are a growing number of middle income families who are now struggling. Families who may have been able to survive on two incomes can begin to struggle quite quickly when one of those is lost. These families can find it very hard to accept that assistance is needed. They may not even know that such help is available to them.

Whilst this is still a rarity it is important that, in dealing with all families, practitioners do not allow an unconscious bias to creep in. That is, not judging someone overtly; rather, it is that as a practitioner we make decisions and assumptions about people based on our own view of the world. People, in our own view, or map of the world, fit into categories that we have long ago decided. As students we are taught to be aware of our unconscious bias and to be mindful of its impact. Unfortunately, as busy practitioners it can be very difficult to keep it in check and it is something that must be continually practiced. As professionals, we all want to fill out the safeguarding jigsaw and we are aware of the pieces that we need in order to complete it. When the jigsaw is finished and we take a step back to look at it, it is important that we remember to check our own personal views before we make any judgments. Every person's view of the completed jigsaw will look somewhat differently depending upon where they are standing when they view it. It will also depend upon the pieces which have been put together and whether or not the jigsaw is fully complete.

The Child in Need process may be the final piece of a jigsaw for some families.

The process works in that a local authority will have done its Section 47 Enquiry and will have reached a conclusion that further involvement of the local authority is needed. It will set up a meeting and, at that meeting, the local authority and other professionals will determine what support or work needs to happen in order to meet those children's needs.

The intervention may be very minimal. It may be that a family needs funding in the short-term in order to assist it. It may be that providing assistance by way of decluttering can be the turning point for a family to make sure that a child's needs are being met.

The Child in Need process will keep the child's welfare needs under review.

In the event that the reviews are positive and the family no longer requires assistance from the local authority, the case will be closed and the local authority will no longer be involved with the family.

In the event that the involvement on a Child in Need basis does not assist the family, the local authority will consider whether or not further intervention is required. This can include the next step which would be child protection plans for the children.

The professionals involved in the Child in Need process are predominantly the local authority. School and health will also play a part in providing their pieces of the jigsaw to the local authority. They should be sharing information around attendance and other key issues which will have been raised as part of key points for the Child in Need process. It is their responsibility to inform the local authority if key steps that have been identified, and for which they are responsible, have not been followed. They are also responsible for informing the local authority if they become aware that parents or carers are not fulfilling their parts of the agreement.

Key points

- The local authority will take the lead.
- Each agency involved with the family can be asked to provide assistance.
- Keep the local authority up to date with parents' engagement in the process.
- Work with other agencies to allow the welfare needs of the child to be met.
- You have a responsibility.

8 CHILD PROTECTION CONFERENCES

A child protection conference is a significant step. It means that a local authority feels there needs to be multi-agency involvement with the family and a plan in place to protect the child.

Child protection conferences can be requested at any time after a strategy meeting or s47 investigation. However, one must be requested when worries that significant harm is being caused are confirmed and the child is suffering, or is likely to suffer, significant harm.

There are helpful flowcharts which you can find at www.kateyoung.org/jigsaw that cover the child protection and conference processes.

There are key timings which should be stuck to. A child protection conference should occur within 15 days of the strategy meeting. That same timescale applies when a local authority is told a child, currently subject to a child protection plan, has moved in to their area,

The purpose of the child protection conference is to decide:

1. Whether or not a child should be made subject to a child protection plan,
2. The basis/category for the plan.
3. The terms of the plan.

Not everyone involved with the family will be invited or required to attend the child protection conference. The main persons required to attend will be:

- Social worker
- School safeguarding lead

- School teacher
- Health visitor (depending on the child's age)
- GP
- Police

If your job title is not listed here, the chances are you will not be asked to attend. Remember, however, that each case is looked at individually. If you are a key person in the child's life you may well be asked to attend and give a view.

It should also be noted that the conference will look at the family as a whole. If there are other children within the family (whether or not they are living with parents or in another household) they can be considered at conference. Remember, each of the other family members will hold part of the family jigsaw. The other children's needs may be the same as the child at conference. It is important to look holistically at the family, rather than as separate members. Sometimes, it is only when you look at what is happening to the family as a whole that you see a clear way forward, or an explanation for the safeguarding situation.

The conference is chaired by the Independent Reviewing Officer (IRO). They are also known as Independent Case Reviewing Officers (ICRO). They have the same function, regardless of title. The IRO Chairs the meeting. They will represent and protect the best interest of the child or children who are the subject of the conference. The IRO is a registered professional with the Health and Care Professionals Council (HCPC), and their background is usually as a child protection social worker.

The location of the conference is important. It needs to be in a room suitable to hold the number of professionals attending, as well as parents. Conferences are usually held in social work offices. Occasionally they are held in schools, depending on the needs of the people attending.

You may find parents want to have lawyers with them. This can be worrying, and you may be cautious about your answers or worried they will try to cross-examine you. Rest assured, a lawyer's role in a child protection conference is limited. They cannot and should not ask you questions. They can remind or prompt their clients, but no more than that. Usually, the lawyer present is a trainee or newly qualified solicitor who will be taking notes of the meeting to discuss later with their client.

If you are asked to attend the child protection conference, you will be asked to provide a short report. The IRO will usually ask for certain information on a standard form. To assist, I have set out each field with some guidance on what to include in your report for the conference.

Health

You will need to advise of any medical conditions, details of any missed appointments, and whether or not any explanations have been provided.

The conference may be seeking information on several aspects of the child's health; for example, GP appointments, diagnoses, dental or eye issues. Usually the conference will want to know about a parent's engagement with those professionals.

Perhaps there are issues with drug misuse. Your report should contain concerns about a parent's presentation at a meeting or appointment. If you are their drug worker, are they engaging for the required drug tests? And what are the results of those tests?

Education

You will be asked to provide information on attendance and punctuality. Please do not just send across the attendance register. The other agencies will not be able to read it easily and it does not alert anyone else to any emerging or established patterns of attendance or punctuality.

Presentation and attainment will also be key areas for the conference. Interaction with other students may also be useful to know. Are they quiet? Angry? Prone to aggression? How about how well they are achieving? Also consider how they look. By this, I mean do they come to school clean in a clean uniform or clothes? Or, perhaps they attend looking unkempt, dirty and in unwashed clothes? Is this having an impact on them? Are they being bullied as a result? What have you tried with parents to resolve the issue?

These are in no way exhaustive lists, but rather some pointers to consider. Each child is different and what is normal for one child will be entirely out of character for another. You hold those pieces of the jigsaw. Is it natural behaviour for them or totally out of character?

For all professionals, also include what you feel the other agencies need to be aware of. Remember, you may be the only person with that knowledge. You hold that piece of the jigsaw.

The conference

The conference itself will roughly take the following structure:

1. The IRO will request reports prior to the conference. These reports will need to be submitted in advance of the conference.

2. Before the conference starts, the IRO will talk to parents and explain how the meeting will work. They will check that parents have received and read the reports from the professionals.

3. One everyone is in the room and around the table, the IRO will ask everyone to introduce themselves.

4. The IRO will set out the purpose of the meeting and note any apologies.

5. The IRO will then invite the professionals, in turn, to raise their concerns. This usually starts with the social worker outlining what the concerns are, to get to the point of needing to have conference. Once that has been explained, questions can be asked and then the IRO will go around the table asking for any updates to reports or clarification of points within a report.

6. Parents will be invited to respond to comments made.

At the end of the discussion, all the professionals will be asked to say whether or not they are of the view the child or children should be subject to a plan.

If it is agreed that a plan is needed, the IRO will invite the professionals and parents to agree on what it should include. The social worker will be the key worker to have control of the plan and to ensure it is developed and adhered to.

A core group of professionals will be put together. This core group can include anyone who was at the conference and any family members who are required to contribute toward the child protection plan. This core group will meet, initially, within 10 days of the conference. They will then meet at least monthly thereafter. The frequency and location for the meetings will be set at the first core group meeting.

The IRO will also set a date for the first review conference. This is usually within three months for a first review and then at six-monthly intervals. This can be different depending on your local practice.

The plan

The child protection plan can include practically anything. Plans often cover requirements for:

- Attendance at school or nursery.
- Attending medical appointments (for parents as well as children, depending on the circumstances).
- Engagement in group work; for example, domestic abuse programmes, strengthening families work, parenting programmes etc.
- Requirements to report incidents to the police or have safety equipment fitted.
- Work with family support workers around safety in the home, cleanliness, budgeting etc.
- What support other professionals will be providing.
- The level of home visits.
- Agreements around seeing the children, and contact arrangements for non-resident carers, such as fathers or grandparents.
- What support the extended family can provide.

As I say, this list is not exhaustive. Each plan should be individual to that particular child. Even within sibling groups, plans can differ to accommodate the individual needs of the children.

Any breaches of the plan that you become aware of should be reported to the key social worker. This will help them put together the jigsaw for that particular child and plan.

Key points

- A conference is held when the concerns that a child is at risk of significant harm are confirmed.
- Each professional who is significantly involved with the

child or family can be asked to attend.
- Professionals attending the conference will be asked for a report.
- After the discussion at conference, the panel will decide whether or not a plan is needed.
- If a plan is needed, the professionals and parents will discuss the content of the plan at the conference.
- A core group of professionals and family members will be set up.
- Continuous sharing of information will help establish whether or not the plan is being stuck to and is working.

9 PUBLIC LAW OUTLINE PROCESS

If the child protection plan resolves matters, the child can be removed from the plan and that may be the end of local authority involvement.

If the plan does not resolve the situation the local authority will look to the next stage of the process.

The next stage is the last stage before a local authority looks at care proceedings. Given the very strict timescales now put in place for court proceedings, this is often the last chance parents or carers have to prove they are able to meet their child's needs.

The Public Law Outline process (PLO, or pre-proceedings stage) can be vital. From a local authority point of view, it is their last chance to work with the family and emphasise how important it is they step up and engage.

For parents, this stage is their last chance to show they are working with the local authority and are able to do what is needed. It is often the first time they will have had legal advice on their particular situation. Many parents do not seek legal advice until they are told that the local authority is proceeding down this route.

PLO letter

The PLO stage starts with legal advice about whether or not the threshold for proceedings has been crossed. Go back to the section on 'Where we are headed' for more information on threshold.

If it is agreed that the threshold for proceedings has been crossed, then the social worker will produce a PLO letter.

Parents need this letter to obtain free legal advice.

The PLO letter sets out all the concerns there are. It will detail the concerns, the action taken by the local authority or other organisations, and whether parents have engaged. Some letters set out this information chronologically. Others use different headings to set out the information. Whatever the format, the purpose is still the same: what are the concerns, what has been done and what has not worked?

It is likely that when this letter is being produced you will be asked for information. This is particularly true if you have been significantly involved with the family, either through education, group work or health (such as drug or alcohol work).

The meeting

The PLO letter will set a date for the first meeting.

At this meeting the local authority, the parents and legal representatives will be in attendance. The meeting is chaired by the social work team or group manager. The social worker will be asked to set out the concerns and provide any updates. This is similar to what happens at the child protection conference.

Parents have an opportunity to share their views and ask for any help they feel they need from the local authority.

The agreement

It is important to remember that, at this stage, parents really need to engage with the local authority. They are only one step away from proceedings and the local authority could be asking the court to remove the children from their parents (if this has not already happened on a voluntary basis). Ultimately, the local authority is holding an awful lot of the cards at this stage in the child protection process.

Parents will need to fully engage, do all the work required of them, and be able to show they have heard what is needed of them and demonstrated they can do it. Half attempts will not be enough at this stage.

As this stage is the last chance before court, it is vital that the social worker has all the pieces of the jigsaw they need. Any missed or late appointments may show a continuing pattern. Late attendances at school, lack of suitable clothing, or further disclosures from children about adults who should not be at the home, may be vital.

As with all the stages we have looked at, the information you are providing, and your piece of the jigsaw, is ever important. It is likely at this stage that parents may ask you not to report, or to allow them time to sort things. Sadly, they are likely to have run out of time.

None of this is intended to set people up to fail, The focus is on the needs of the child.

The agreement will be specific about what the parents need to do in order to stop the local authority issuing proceedings. Failing on just one point of the plan could see the local authority issuing proceedings. Parents will be given time at the end of the meeting to take legal advice on the agreement being proposed. There is some wiggle room within the agreement for parents, but not a lot. Parents and the social work manager will sign the agreement.

The manager will set a date for the review meeting. This is usually within three months. The whole PLO process is a short, sharp intervention. It should last no longer than six months, and certainly no longer than 12 months.

If the local authority does go into court, the agreement will be used as evidence that the threshold has been crossed and the child was, or is still, at risk of significant harm.

If this seems a little harsh, remember that this meeting is taking place after a significant amount of work and involvement of the local authority and other professionals.

The social worker will not share the agreement with other professionals in its entirely. They should, however, alert you to any elements where your organisation will be asked to provide feedback. If you are in any doubt about what you are being asked, check with the social worker as to what exactly is being sought.

Key points

- This is the last stage before court proceedings.
- The PLO letter will set out the concerns the local authority has.
- An agreement will be signed by parents and social work manager.
- It must be adhered to.
- If it is broken, the local authority can use the agreement as evidence in court proceedings.

10 CARE PROCEEDINGS

In Chapter 3, 'Where are we headed?', we looked at the potential outcome if all other child protection processes fail.

If none of the other child protection processes succeed at improving the parent's ability to meet the child's needs then consideration will be given to court proceedings.

You will remember that in Chapter 3 we looked at the requirements for court proceedings. If the concerns are still present then a social worker will contact their in-house legal team to find out if they have enough evidence to go to court. This is called the threshold for proceedings. The threshold is set out in s31(2) Children Act 1989. It says:

(2) A court may only make a care order or supervision order if it is satisfied—
(a) that the child concerned is suffering, or is likely to suffer, significant harm; and
(b) that the harm, or likelihood of harm, is attributable to—
(i) the care given to the child, or likely to be given to him if the order were not made, not being what it would be reasonable to expect a parent to give to him; or
(ii) the child's being beyond parental control.

If the decision is that the threshold criteria has been met, as above, then the local authority will look to go to court for a court order. That order could be to share parental responsibility (a care order) and give the local authority more say in a child's life than the parents. The order could also be to befriend and assist the child (a supervision order). There could also be no order (sometimes used when legal judgements need to be made but no order is necessary).

Whatever the reason, it is a very serious step.

What are care proceedings?

Care proceedings happen when a local authority makes an application to the court because there are concerns that a child or children within a family are at significant risk of harm and the local authority is seeking to share parental responsibility.

A local authority can apply for a couple of orders. These are:

Care order – this will allow a local authority to share parental responsibility with parents or other care givers. A care order grants a local authority over arching parental responsibility, this means they can make decisions for a child, even if parents don't agree.

Supervision order – this allows a local authority to advise, assist and befriend the child or children who are the subject of the order. It is used a lot where there is a family placement and support will be needed to help with contact.

If a local authority is successful in its application for a care order, it will look at long term care for the child. This may be with a family member. Such placements can be supported with a supervision order.

A child may be placed under a Child Arrangements Order or a Special Guardianship Order. A Child Arrangements Order will confirm where a child is to live or with whom they are to have contact. In this book I am looking only at those cases where this order says where a child is to live. A Child Arrangements Order confirming where a child lives will give the carer parental responsibility.

Many of you will know what parental responsibility is. I'm conscious I've used that term several times now. To be clear, parental responsibility is the responsibility given to a caregiver to make key decisions in a child's life. Decisions on education, health care, where they live and day to day care are the main ones. People who have parental responsibility for a child will have been invited to previous meetings about the child's welfare needs.

Timescales

When a local authority makes an application for a care order there is a strict structure to follow. That structure sets out, in law, that care proceedings should be finished within 26 weeks. Every step of the process is set out in a flow chart and in legislation. You can download the flowchart at www.kateyoung.org/jigsaw.

I appreciate that some of you will never be involved in care proceedings. However, it is likely you will be on edge of the process. As such, knowing how it works and what is needed when can be really helpful.

It is useful to start by saying that every court has a slightly different way of running this process. That said, every set of proceedings should follow the procedure I've set out below.

The first step is that the local authority will make an application for an order. To support that application a social worker will prepare the following documentation:

- Statement
- Care plan – for each of the children subject of the application
- Chronology
- Genogram

The social worker will send to their legal team the following documentation:

- All assessments previously completed, for example;
    - Parenting assessments
    - Connected carers assessments
    - S47 assessments
    - PLO letters
- Any reports from professionals which support their application for example:
    - School
    - Health – GP and health visitor
    - Medical reports from consultants

These lists are not exhaustive.

The court timetable starts when the local authority files its application with the court and the court issues it.

Day 1 happens when the local authority's application is issued by the court. That is a formal process that happens by way of paper exercise within the court office.

By **Day 2**, the documents that the local authority is using in support of its application at that very early stage are all sent through to the Independent Children's Guardian's body and The Children and Family Court Advisory and Support Service, or in short CAFCAS, and a Children's Guardian is appointed for the child or children. Briefly, the Children's Guardian is there to represent the child or children's best interests within these court proceedings. They will see the children and, depending on their age, they will have a chat with them, find out what it is they want, they will talk to parents and, before the first hearing, they will provide to the court an initial analysis. That initial analysis is of the evidence that's been filed and of their discussions with parents.

When the local authority issues its application, all of this evidence potentially is there, so that could involve statements from you, depending on your sector. It could involve police information, health information, and a statement from the social worker, and definitely a chronology and care plans for the child or children if the local authority is looking to share parental responsibility and potentially remove a child from his/her family.

Less than three weeks later, the court will have its first hearing in relation to the case and at that first hearing the court will agree and tell everybody what will happen next, which usually involves what further evidence needs to be filed with the court. This information is required by the court in order for a Judge to make a decision about the local authority's application.

Between the first date, the day the court issues the proceedings, and that first hearing, the parents will get copies of all the information and they should go and get legal advice. All the solicitors get together before that first hearing and look at what evidence is there and decide what further information needs to be put before the court. This further evidence might look at expert witnesses and, depending upon the circumstances, may include looking at a psychiatrist's report if there are mental health concerns, or a psychologist, maybe looking at risk assessments depending on the particular facts of that case. If it went in quickly there will be a lot of information required and you, as a person who works with that child, may be asked to provide a report. So if you work for a school and you're their teacher, you might be asked to provide a report, or a nursery may be asked to provide a report.

If proceedings have been issued because of an injury to a child, then health professionals (possibly a consultant) will be asked to provide a report. If the child has been presented at school and/or nursery, they will be asked to say how the child presented and what was happening and what was going on at that stage.

This all happens and all these decisions are made within that three week period.

At the first court hearing (by **Day 18**), the Judge will look at what evidence is there and will either accept it or reject the information and seek further evidence. Now remember, the local authority has to prove its case that a child is at risk of significant harm, and that information could be historical information relating to a parent as well, so that can take some time to get hold of and sometimes you have not been able to get that beforehand because a parent has not agreed to it being shared with the local authority if it is about them.

If you're involved with a parent and that information has not been agreed to be shared and you have not been involved prior, there may be an Order asking you to send that information to the local authority so it can be shared with everybody. Even if you have provided a report to the local authority in the early stages, you might be asked for an update, particularly if you have done work with the parents. For example, you might be asked to update that information. If you have done some drug testing and drug work with them, then you will be asked to update that. If they have been missing appointments, then you might be asked to provide an updated statement in terms of whether or not they have been attending and how that's going.

All of that information has to be gathered before the court can make its ultimate decision.

Now, unless there are any problems after that first hearing, which is just under three weeks later, the next hearing won't take place until week 20.

In just over three months – about 17 weeks – all assessments, all expert evidence, all the local authority's final statements, and all final decisions around that evidence by a local authority have to be made and parents have to respond to that information, as does the Guardian as an independent person looking out for the child's best interests. That means that if parents want to demonstrate they have changed, they have about 12 weeks to show it. That is not a long time.

If you are a professional involved with the family, the local authority is going to want your information within that timeframe. If you have just become involved with a family, or maybe you have known them for a while, you might be asked to express an opinion about whether or not they're able to do this. The cut-off point is a short period of time, just 12 weeks (three months), and sometimes it is much shorter than that. It is that period when a local authority will need all the information in.

If a local authority writes to you and asks for information, it really does need a very quick response. If you cannot get the information, or if you need further information or a court order, you need to tell the local authority that is what you need. Any delay will have an impact in terms of having all the evidence together for the court and potentially putting a child at risk.

In an ideal world, all of these assessments should have been done at the beginning, before the proceedings start. It is not unusual for parents start to show some level of change and some level of understanding at the court door. The information requested from you needs to be provided to the local authority really quickly. This is because the local authority has to think about what you have said, it has to look at your information with everything else that it has got, and analyse it.

The hearing after the hearing in week three should be the Issues Resolution Hearing. There can be a couple of hearings before this stage to make sure the court has everything it needs. This is usually the case when a child has suffered an injury and the court has to manage a number of expert reports. At each stage of the court process, the Judge will manage what evidence is filed with the court and when.

At the Issues Resolution Hearing, the court has to decide whether or not it has all the information it needs to make a final decision. It is also at this hearing when the court will expect the lawyers to decide what issues it needs to resolve at the final hearing. The court will decide what witnesses are needed for the final hearing. If you have prepared a report for court then you may be asked to come and give evidence to the court about your report.

At the final hearing, decisions will be made about the child's future. The court will consider all the evidence before it and make that decision.

Court proceedings are difficult and stressful for everyone involved. Even after it has all ended, the decisions made can have lifelong consequences for parents and children. Ultimately, the court is looking to make the right welfare decision for a child. These are rarely easy.

It is precisely because the consequences can be life changing, that court proceedings are the last resort of the local authority. Each piece of the jigsaw should come together during these proceedings to allow a Judge to see the whole picture when making their decision.

Key points

- A local authority must have evidence that the threshold has been crossed before it can start court proceedings.
- When court proceedings start, the court will set the

timetable.
- Your reports many be used as evidence to support the local authority's case.
- You may be asked to provide a further report or update to the court. Timescales may be really tight.
- The court will consider all the evidence before it comes to any decisions.

CONCLUSION

Child protection processes are difficult. They can also be intimidating, particularly if you are new to the whole process.

Every step taken, from referral through to court proceedings, is an intervention into family life. Some of the families involved will be welcoming of help. Most, however, won't. Your piece of the jigsaw will sometimes feel very hard to share. You may feel intimidated by colleagues or from the family to keep your piece hidden or not show the whole piece. You will see through this book how vital your piece of the jigsaw may be. Without your piece of the jigsaw no-one throughout the whole child protection process will see the full picture.

Sharing information is vital to the whole jigsaw being seen. Information should be shared continually. Your individual picture will change constantly. Lives are never static, even the most regulated life will have nuances. Those nuances continually colour your piece of the jigsaw.

ABOUT THE AUTHOR

Kate Young is a qualified child protection lawyer who specialises in helping safeguarding professionals in all aspects of their role.

Kate works with social workers, early years practitioners and many others through training, coaching and online courses. The Safeguarding Academy is where all these professionals come together to share best practice, find all the safeguarding documents in one place, and get monthly training videos and workbooks.

Content Disclaimer
The information contained in this book is provided for information purposes only. The contents of this book are not intended to amount to advice and you should not rely on any of the contents of this book. Professional advice should be obtained before taking or refraining from taking any action as a result of the contents of this book. Katherine T Young Ltd & Kate Young disclaims all liability and responsibility arising from any reliance placed on any of the contents of this book.

Made in the USA
Charleston, SC
21 November 2016